# I Will Miss Kindergarten

Written by Miles Muchemi

Illustrated by Tullip Studio

Copyright © 2022 Miles Muchemi and Yolanda T. Marshall

All rights reserved. No portion of this book may be reproduced without permission from the publisher, except as permitted by U.S. and Canadian copyright laws. This book is based on a documented and publicly shared speech by the author in 2021.
For permissions, contact: GarnalmaPress@gmail.com
Editor: Yolanda T. Marshall

*I am dedicating this book to my beautiful mom, who reads to me every night. And to my excellent kindergarten teachers, Mrs Richardson and Mrs Myers.*

Hi, I'm Miles,
and I enjoyed kindergarten

I had two great teachers who had a Caribbean accent like Grandma.

I will miss my teachers, and I will miss my friends.

But some of them will be in the new classroom with me.

I love to read.
My mother and teachers always encouraged and helped me.

Now I read like a grade-two student.

When I grow up, I want to be a judge. I want to put bad people in jail and prevent innocent people from going to jail.

I'm going to miss kindergarten.

I played as much as I had to work, which was absolutely awesome!

Goodbye, kindergarten.
Grade one, here I come!

The beginning...